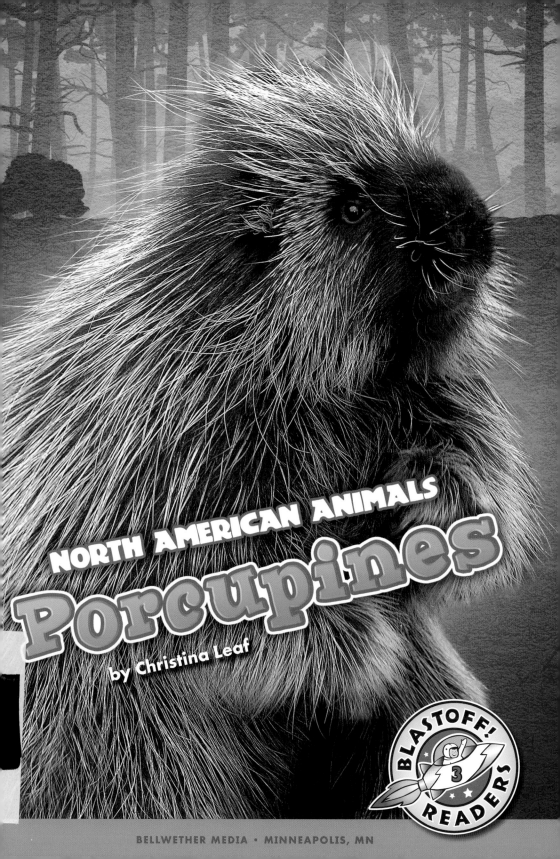

NORTH AMERICAN ANIMALS

Porcupines

by Christina Leaf

BLASTOFF! READERS
3

BELLWETHER MEDIA • MINNEAPOLIS, MN

Note to Librarians, Teachers, and Parents:

Blastoff! Readers are carefully developed by literacy experts and combine standards-based content with developmentally appropriate text.

Level 1 provides the most support through repetition of high-frequency words, light text, predictable sentence patterns, and strong visual support.

Level 2 offers early readers a bit more challenge through varied simple sentences, increased text load, and less repetition of high-frequency words.

Level 3 advances early-fluent readers toward fluency through increased text and concept load, less reliance on visuals, longer sentences, and more literary language.

Level 4 builds reading stamina by providing more text per page, increased use of punctuation, greater variation in sentence patterns, and increasingly challenging vocabulary.

Level 5 encourages children to move from "learning to read" to "reading to learn" by providing even more text, varied writing styles, and less familiar topics.

Whichever book is right for your reader, Blastoff! Readers are the perfect books to build confidence and encourage a love of reading that will last a lifetime!

This edition first published in 2016 by Bellwether Media, Inc.

No part of this publication may be reproduced in whole or in part without written permission of the publisher. For information regarding permission, write to Bellwether Media, Inc., Attention: Permissions Department, 5357 Penn Avenue South, Minneapolis, MN 55419.

Library of Congress Cataloging-in-Publication Data

Leaf, Christina.
  Porcupines / by Christina Leaf.
    pages cm. – (Blastoff! Readers. North American Animals)
Summary: "Simple text and full-color photography introduce beginning readers to porcupines. Developed by literacy experts for students in kindergarten through third grade"– Provided by publisher.
  Audience: Ages 5-8
  Audience: K to grade 3
  Includes bibliographical references and index.
    ISBN 978-1-62617-262-3 (hardcover: alk. paper)
1. Porcupines–Juvenile literature. I. Title.
QL737.R652L43 2016
  599.35'97–dc23
                                        2014050319

Table of Contents

What Are Porcupines?

Porcupines are spiky **rodents**. These **mammals** live across much of Canada and the western United States.

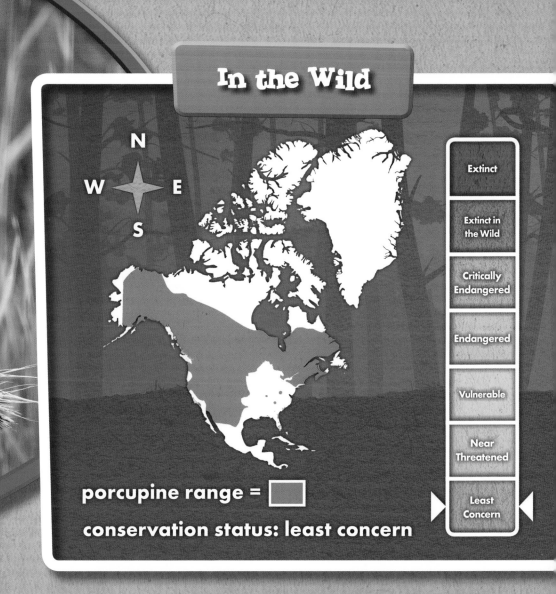

In the Wild

N
W · E
S

Extinct

Extinct in the Wild

Critically Endangered

Endangered

Vulnerable

Near Threatened

Least Concern

porcupine range =

conservation status: least concern

Most porcupines make homes in forests. Some porcupines roam western **scrublands**. In the north, they may live in **tundra**.

Porcupines have brown or black fur. They are also covered in sharp **quills**. These quills are dark with white tips.

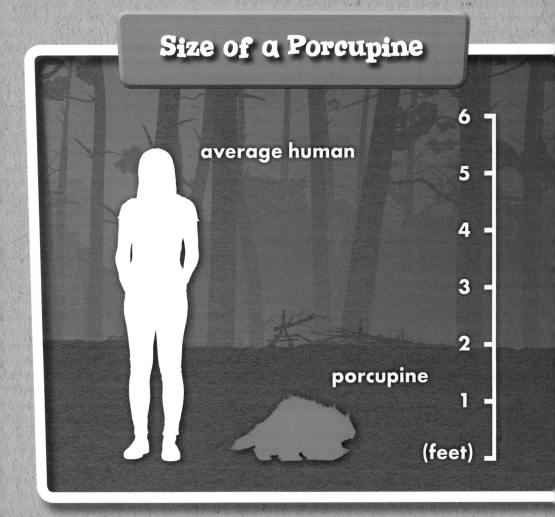

Size of a Porcupine

average human

6

5

4

3

2

porcupine

1

(feet)

Male porcupines are larger than females. They can weigh up to 35 pounds (16 kilograms). Most porcupines measure just over 2 feet (0.6 meters) in length.

quills rough foot pads long claws

Porcupines usually live high in trees. Long claws and rough pads on their feet help them climb.

In pine forests or open areas, porcupines make **dens** in **hollow** logs or underground.

Finding Food

Porcupines **forage** at night. They look for food in trees or on the ground.

On the Menu

hemlock bark

spruce needles

acorns

yellow water lilies

sugar maple buds

raspberry leaves

Leaves and tree buds are favorite treats. Porcupines also nibble on flowers, berries, and nuts.

Some porcupines eat plants from lakes or streams. They swim to find this food. Their quills help them float.

In winter, food can be hard to find. Then these **herbivores** chew on bark and pine needles.

Facing Enemies

Few **predators** hunt porcupines. The spiky animals are protected by strong **defenses**.

mountain lions

bobcats

grizzly bears

gray wolves

great horned owls

fishers

When porcupines sense danger, they click their teeth as a warning. They raise their quills if this does not work.

When a predator comes too close, the porcupine hits it with its tail. The sharp quills stick in the animal.

Barbs make the quills hard to pull out.

Porcupettes

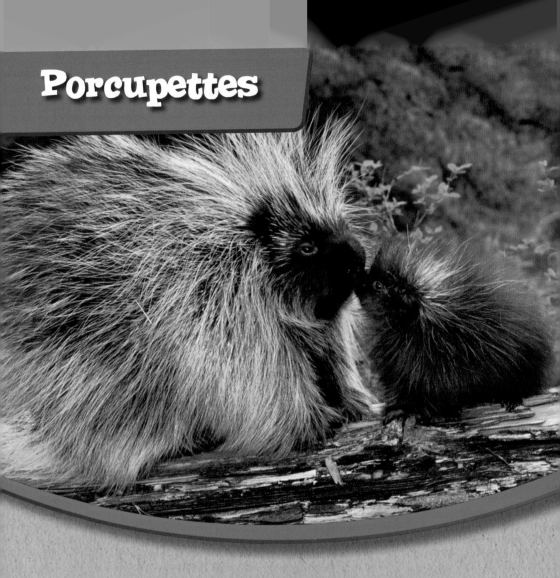

In spring, a female porcupine has one baby. A **porcupette** is born with soft quills. These harden after about an hour. Mom hides her baby on the ground. It cannot climb trees yet.

Baby Facts

Name for babies:	porcupettes
Size of litter:	1 porcupette
Length of pregnancy:	7 months
Time spent with mom:	6 months

At first, the porcupette **nurses**.
Then it forages with mom at night.

After six months, the
young porcupine goes
off on its own!

Glossary

barbs—sharp hooks that point backward and make quills hard to remove

defenses—ways of keeping an animal safe

dens—sheltered places; porcupines build dens in caves or in hollow logs or trees.

forage—to go out in search of food

herbivores—animals that only eat plants

hollow—empty through the middle

mammals—warm-blooded animals that have backbones and feed their young milk

nurses—drinks mom's milk

porcupette—a baby porcupine

predators—animals that hunt other animals for food

quills—sharp, hollow spines on a porcupine

rodents—small animals that gnaw on their food

scrublands—dry lands with short bushes and trees

tundra—dry land where the ground is frozen year-round

To Learn More

AT THE LIBRARY

Antill, Sara. *Porcupines*. New York, N.Y.: Windmill Books, 2011.

Rockwood, Leigh. *Tell Me the Difference Between a Porcupine and a Hedgehog*. New York, N.Y.: PowerKids Press, 2013.

Webster, Christine. *Porcupines*. New York, N.Y.: Weigl, 2010.

ON THE WEB
Learning more about porcupines is as easy as 1, 2, 3.

1. Go to www.factsurfer.com.

2. Enter "porcupines" into the search box.

3. Click the "Surf" button and you will see a list of related web sites.

With factsurfer.com, finding more information is just a click away.

Index

The images in this book are reproduced through the courtesy of: Don Johnston/ Age Fotostock, front cover; Lynn Bystrom, pp. 4-5; Jason Ondreicka, p. 6; Critterbiz, p. 8 (top left); Eric Isselee, p. 8 (top middle, bottom); A_Lein, p. 8 (top right); ARCO/ Henry, P./ Glow Images, p. 9; Tony Rix, pp. 10-11; Timothy Epp, p. 11 (top left); markiss, p. 11 (top right); Hurst Photo, p. 11 (middle left); noppharat, p. 11 (middle right); Alexandr Makarov, p. 11 (bottom left); Dima Sobko, p. 11 (bottom right); Doug Lindstrand/ Corbis, pp. 12-13; Michael S. Quinton/ Exactostock-1701/ Superstock, p. 13; P. Henry/ Glow Images, pp. 14-15; Ultrashock, p. 15 (top left); Svetlana Foote, p. 15 (top right); Nagel Photography, p. 15 (middle left); Maxim Kulko, p. 15 (middle right); mlorenz, p. 15 (bottom left); Holly Kuchera, p. 15 (bottom right); Michelle Gilders/ Alamy, p. 16; Ron Sanford/ Corbis, p. 17; Tom & Pat Leeson/ a/ Age Fotostock, pp. 18-19; Holly Kuchera, p. 19; Tom Brakefield/ Exactostock-1555/ Superstock, pp. 20-21; JohnPitcher, p. 21.